A Deeper Evolution of Reflection

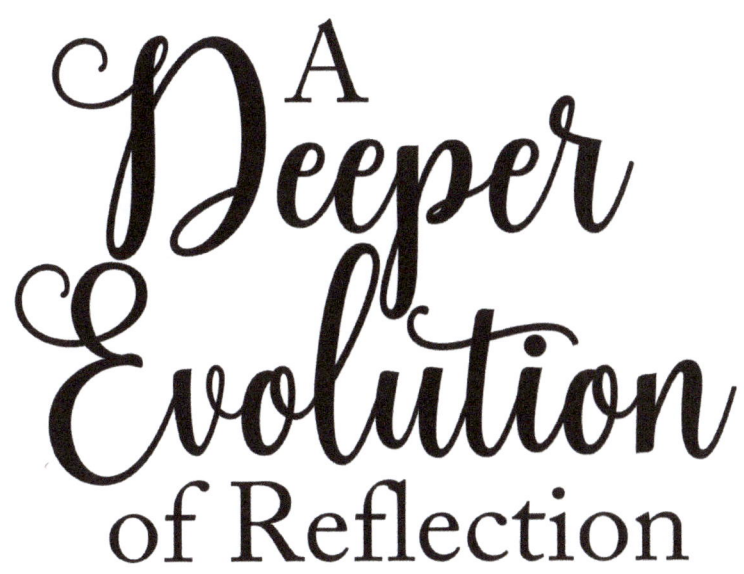

A Deeper Evolution of Reflection

PERRY DOUGLAS SISK

PRIMIX
PUBLISHING
THE WRITE CHOICE

Primix Publishing
East Brunswick Office Evolution
1 Tower Center Boulevard, Ste 1510
East Brunswick, NJ 08816
www.primixpublishing.com
Phone: 1-800-538-5788

Published by Primix Publishing: 04/22/2025

ISBN: 979-8-89194-455-8(sc)
ISBN: 979-8-89194-456-5(hc)
ISBN: 979-8-89194-457-2(e)

Library of Congress Control Number: 2025905412

Contents

A better reason -- Perry d sisk

November O 24

There is a time that we are given to get things done in relation
to a season

As in that time in which we were young and refused advice of
Elders

Just For No Good Reason

All that arrogance of youth yes we thought we knew it all

Given what lie ahead and refused to hear the call

That call to listen close and take heed of Lessons Learned

Experienced by those so older look back to what they had burned

Those bridges they did cross never thinking of a loss

 of what they wished they'd kept

And rather with no thought did they toss

Yes in time we come to know those steps we did not take

Compared to others failed or succeeded

By choices they did make

Pride got in the way at times that sway decision making

Unable to discern that line we cross so fine that left us always shaking

Just how do you best determine what is heavy on our hearts

Were it not for clearly seeing what weighs Upon Our Minds

Is just what sets us all apart

All those things when brought to bare or face

does anyone Wonder just Why We Stand where

Still I feel it is love compassion and Grace

That serves as a cohesion

That substance only seen by actions taken to show

What's been given freely for all a better reason.....

A choice above

perry sisk--jan025

Of all the many things of nature we're entitled to look upon
Such as the many colors of fall
A golden stream a newborn Fawn
So many Treasures there are to behold
Most taken for granted
On our way to becoming old
All too often our thoughts fall short
On seeing where we fail
As seeing old ships at Port
Guided in with Rudder and sail
Those that stand firm on all
they believe in or know
Still looking for signs to affirm or deny
Those things we can't see will show
A life that's been tested and withstood the Heat and the cold
Measured with time not only endurance
In all too short a time becoming old

Ones purpose for being lends to question what for
What is passed on to others
Some strive to ignore
For those willing and hopeful to adhere to his voice
Found reason in living
While holding one choice he comes now the day
To see the doctor and meet that awkward nurse
Forgetting just what chapter though
Holding out to find one verse
That spells it out in simple words
That say just where we're at
Evermore real it now becomes
To know just where we sat
Often at a fork in the road
To choose go left or right
Knowing well what Darkness holds
We still reach for the light
For in this realm of good and warmth we always feel the love
This Spirit of kindness dare we lose
Did we gain from high above.....

A father's need

perry d sisk--feb025

Present day these sounds I hear
these sights i see
i'd like to have depart from me
Far too much to misunderstand
Rather than explain what
has swept across this land
some will call it justice
For the justice that's been lost
Others call it judgment
For our God some people tossed
thrown to the wayside or
solely just abandoned or led away from
A belief that once was held as sacred
our father the spirit and son
As a kid I did ignore those signs
I looked upon not knowing
What was hidden in a song

all the while I'm growing

All things that has been spoken of

Forever put to print

did always hold a hidden message

so few picked up on sent

putting two and two together

Always comes to number four

so simple is a fix to this

to last forevermore

Just say to the one that had given us his son

We are sorry we done wrong

There is no time like the present

To rewrite our hearts in song

a song we sing to praise his name

Again as once before

We walked away and felt the absence

of a love we must restore

as a father loves his children

The reverse is also true

Not so much for why it is needed

for indeed he is needed too.........

A nature of what is true

perry d sisk--feb025

Once again it seems akin
To the pulling of one's teeth
To try and find Don't Look Behind
On high or far beneath

Far and Away some hope to say
They did so follow through
On plans they made though memories fade
Forgetting all that is true

Even seeds planted on flat land or Hills slanted
They all take root and grow
As trees they will splinter
With blizzard Winds of a winter
They too will one day show

Once where they stood in a forest we found wood
To build with or to burn
To cook with or heat those early homes did we cheat
What nature allowed us to learn

Has it not always been the case
in dreams we often Chase
Those ways of getting back
It was kinder to keep in mind
That peace we seldom find
That nature of love we lack..........

A Promise

Perry d Sisk---Jan025

If given the opportunity to cross
the oceans lakes and rivers
would i be given sight in ways
to count by number those deeds that love delivers

If being created in the image of GOD
bares more than what is seen
For in the hearts therein contains
His love in time redeem

One need never question
the how or why or when
The summation of good that dominates
from the message the cross did send

Most of us go on what our sense tell us is real
just as fire will harden and temper
that two edge sword of steel

One that has been ever constant
as the stars in heaven and sun of day
with that ongoing struggle just to get by
or hang on to hope
always this we hear him say
FEAR NOT I AM HERE TO STAY

A reason to part

perry d sisk

things we see and watch that seem to slip away

time alone does hold no candle when it's all broken down some
say

I call it a gift each are given this ability to recall

then too of course it is instilled Within to get up again

each time we take a fall

depending on just who we look at we take that measurement of

call it caliber or character trait

for whatever the case it's love

we must admit that circumstance plays

a grander role for this

where it not for failing to attain one's love

how then can we know to miss

fast approaching those Twilight years that give cause to

dwell on things that's been

some will find Pride in uncovering those things we hide

a way to find again

we that are old who have no one to hold

are prone to miss the most

with Oblivion at the door

and we long forevermore to join our Father the Son and Holy
Ghost,,, amen and amen..........

A score of faith

Perry d sisk--Feb025

If someone said to me
that i am gonna be
that tiny little stone in the hoof
of the horse you ride upon
In other words within a saddle
or in a boat that has no paddle
this trip through life alone while touph
and rocky will one day all be gone

All our long and living years
emersed in wonderment and at times relentless fears
leaves open chances yet to take if only for
avoidance of things we leave at stake

If given foreknowledge of why or our
purpose for simply being
what then would be a reason to expose
those that are blind from those that are seeing

So what if just what if we are all
a part of one greater game of chess
This world is the board we move upon
in the end who's left to guess

So who is to say
with just one dream away
from that answer awaited for

Between the lines
among the ryhmes it is faith
that yields the score........

A spiritual vessel sees

Perry d Sisk--October 024

As I Lay this vessel down tonight

I wait for slumber to bring to light

Perhaps in dreams or visions I'll see

What lies ahead or things that must be

No one holds the future in sight even when darkness yields to light

Some say that a prophet holds some glimmer

Of what has been and what is yet to simmer

I guess it goes without saying sure we plan ahead

But then again just what or even who steps in instead

Always has been one hopeful Outlook on such that may be

But just as those dreams and visions I will just wait on to see

To see if I find as this vessel awakens again

Or my soul God keeps safe should I see a final end

For you see this body and flesh made of clay

My Father in Heaven is also the Potter

Of this vessel his spirit will stay.............

a thought to measure

perry d sisk--feb025

I like reading stories that travel life's road
The Corn and soybean fields
That a farmer had sewed
Catching fish from a pond
from a lake or a stream
those visions of peace
we hold in a dream
trees budding out early in spring
the snow melting away
migrating birds on the wing
reminding were it not for seasons that change
Nothing new would come to pass
No new life on the range
time it moves faster
With each passing year
Regardless letting go dismissing the fear
What falls in between one occurrence or event

Of our lives we have lived and the love of all spent

in minds eye we see there's been nothing in vain

Looking back on it all did we always see rain

This rain put in place to foster anew

has Ben and will be constant

as memories grow few

Far and Between all others we've treasured

which speak for itself

all in one full measure..........

a trust never lost

Perry d sisk---feb025

sitting with my coffee again on another restless morn

all the previous hours of the early AM

once more I find I am sworn

sworn to commit another day fulfill those tasks at hand

Go to the store buy this thing and more

keeping habits just where they stand

I think of things yet left to do

With no set plan on getting through

Sitting here in solitude is just myself that asks

Am I the only one to wear these shoes

I hope their soles will last

It has always taken very little to sustain this way of living

Though all the while I seem to smile for those of which I am giving

as in that old adage it's better to give than Receive

Giving unto others as we wish that all believe

In and of these latter years I have come to see one most important thing

that in my youth I gave no thinking on this wisdom age would bring

living a life in simple ways to exclude a complex world

Does allow that peace of mind and getting by this silver beard now curled

So where did man adopt this nature two love ones neighbor as his self

Was it the one trait given to all or something found upon a higher shelf

If this had always been the case how would he have known

was it something found in place or a picture that was shown

Finding truth among the vast amount of lies

Told over generations as there are clouds among our skies

Find your way forward and forget what falls behind

For all that has been and all of what was that concept keeping us blind

So gaining insights of things that are just

give honor and praise to the creator above

I never lose our trust...

A truth in heart

Perry d Sisk--Jan025

I've seen in pictures
and i have heard in songs
the joys of living
and the many of our wrongs

Are we often taken back
to a time of peace of mind
there too as well reminded
of what roads to take we find

What more is there to witness
or be brought to light to see
with a sun that rises up each day
and sets across the sea

what more we hope to find in life
are things that can't be measured
A heart that holds no conditions
for love this alone is treasured

When someone questions this judgement made
i've not been around this long
without becomming shrewd and strong
with nothing more to trade

this at my years i am most assured of
that the spirit of the father
came down to touch his son
in the form of just a dove

dispute this not for righteous sake
what more of absolution is here to set apart
the one decision we're left to make
is one to take to heart

An end to a story

Perry Sisk-December 024

Something new now comes to mind
I'm sure that others will also find
As a kid in school trying to fit in
Seemed to always be the rule
Like the thumb I'd raise to cars passing by
In hopes that one would stop
And with that I'd sigh
Well that rule of thumb now passed
Into just one more memory
That seems to always last
Lasting past and well beyond
Those years and times with friendships Bond
Some see their future as foretold
By oh so many now found old
As warmth and kindness that is now turned cold
These times we are in predicted to be
With all that we witness and never want to see

With what has been said more is there to dread
Those stories we were told
Now all put to bed
At times our past comes back to haunt and oh so badly
Dare we relinquish our Treasures gladly
For in doing that alone we do resist
in defiance with certainty
Do we raise our fist
You call it protest or say just to deny
No more as being said just take it on the fly
For all is seen these times my friend
With talk of our days so near to an end
What is to say it's a newer starting point
That the father looked down on his children
And saw them out of joint
This I say to one and all
With willingness to hear and heed this call
There is no time like the present to ask him into our hearts
Before it is too late to get back up when we fall
A fall from his grace and Glory
To be said one Ending Story

A color of conviction

Perry d sisk --- Nov O24

We can bang our heads against the wall
And pound our fists upon the table
Yet nothing goes against the grain
As being told we were just not able
Of all the planets there are or may not be
And all the stars at night with those we still can't see
Much in the way of what we hold inside
Our abilities and gifts that we often choose to hide
Not so much from others but so much more from ourselves
Like stories and fables concealed in books
So aligned along their shelves
While it is so true these thoughts are just so simply brought
About by Idle of thinking
But now present day there will be those that say
You're off your meds or it's all in what you're drinking

So never rule out these things that I
have as set apart from others

For indeed the firmament placed
above concealed in Darkness

And in light will one day reveal true colors

Due course

Perry sisk--December 024

What is it that I do when I can't find any rest

Well I get up and stir around as many others do I guess

Searching for my coffee cup like the nosy wanderings of a pup

Somedays it seems I find no surprise in
seeing what was down turned up

Each and every morning of late before
the dawn the Sun that breaks

The light of day between the trees reflects
upon the ponds and lakes

Giving thanks to God above we all should do I reckon

If just to show he's on our minds and
in our hearts that beckon

To the spirit of good and Grace we know we hold inside

Knowing well we are here to tell

One truth that all confide

A life that drove you down so low

You're made to look up to see the underside

What picture will be painted

As time and events will fall away
Was it said of man whose Hearts had fainted
As his son comes back one day

finding home

perry d sisk--feb025

Found in the stillness once again
Of late it seems so common for me
less time to dream or so it would seem
it is all just meant to be
I recall being told one day
I'd be old and look back on things I'll miss
The warmth of middle day
those kids all at play
that time of utter bliss
of course knowing then what now I'm finding thin
this time remaining will not hold
The Signs that I wear
This gray and silver hair
a mirror that says I'm old
This goes without saying Each day I am praying
To hang around to see what's new
with any new dawn the Green of a lawn

A cloudless sky of blue

These thoughts here are simple and plain as anyone can see

The what it says to you as well as others too

that time is Short for me

to have some word said on paper instead

or annoying someone that hears

Some thoughts of just one

that weights on the son To abolish all his fears

No one can dismiss what the young will resist

That one moment we are alone

As we sit in that chair

Or stand knowing where

so destined to be called home.....

In absence of what may have been

Where was it ever said one must leave the boundaries we were placed as shown
Some never leave their place of birth or go very far from home
As for myself I have not traveled far
A few states away I would roam

Aside from vocation there was no predication
That called for much at all
We all hold the choice and given a voice
To say no to answer a call

Then some will do as others have done
To escape that Destiny of fate
So little will we ever know
It shall always happen late

What are we hearing from the so called prophets this day

Be ready for what is coming repent ye now and walk your path this way

Nothing I find can be worse out of life
than looking back and wishing
I had done that different now knowing what I know
To see what all that I was missing..........

one beach to walk

perry d sisk--feb025

Back in the days when the Pegasus seemed real
and all the mythology since Ingrained in fables
and Stories that steal
stealing imaginations away from the young
and seeing how kids in school
missed a bell that had rung
Ringing out to all that would hear one day
would come a voice to some be so clear
What speaks of one day there will be
So many called on to say
this time is at hand what comes to fruition
is love in our hearts
one long lasting condition
it all seems never ending
these questions we raise
though all the while Telling ourselves
Who it is we should praise

praise for the one that made us unique

In ways like the clouds that surround a mountain peak

So many that walk in and out of our lives

They seem to leave traces

Of a purpose that drives

Driving us on and forward to reach

That pathway we find on one Sandy Beach

That Sand we walk On some firm and some soft

We gaze across the waters

and See birds high aloft

as they touch that part of Heaven

Always there we can't see

With all that we imagine

Do Angels walk behind me........

One message of Grace

perry d sisk--jan025

If Ever I find favor enough
To clasp the hand of all that is made
What then would be left to ponder
or ever have been answered
For this life it took to trade
Where finds one and inspiration to ever carry on
Beyond what dreams reveal
So in Tarry not the hours to awaken from
To show whose reality is real
For reaching vision from where we are to reflect
What has been or yet will be
Call it a gift or just random Talent
To express to any to see
Reminds me of a story
Of a once misguided soul
Yet to be placed inside one man
Called on to pay a toll

Ways always shown though hardly ever known
The roads this one did take
And all the times hopeful that his faith would never fail
And so fearful of what is at stake
Imparted in ways that still the Gaze
Of other standing by
That looked upon one Written song
They hold their heads so high
To catch a sight on what takes flight
Upon one's Journeys end
Far to reach what was left to teach
One message left would send.............

One promise to keep

perry d sisk--feb025

I make this declaration
As I see such degradation
Those Visions so held when as a child
Now in such desperation
Desperate to find and hold again
What once was so streamlined
That time back then I see has been
Misguided and refined
Refined into this time we call new
Progressively said to be better
They'll fail to see the obscurity
Of one's heartfelt open letter
Love and Passions of our past
Sought for fashion thought to last
It's one trait so sacred given to all at conception
Never taught or ever learned

One seed yet to be planted our soul with inherent reflection

As sure as a bush that burned

This time to walk on earth is short

Given all we know to accept

To improve upon all that has been

Brings less from all that is kept

Kept in each spirit The Light of Life saves

To disallow our promise

To escape for always our Graves..........

One saving grace

perry d sisk--feb025

One is given insight into
matters yet be known
where or why this trait is derived
from truth or lies once sown

Given such turmoil that abounds
these days sleep is seldom found
with days that grow shorter
and nights that i loiter
for nothing i hear is sound

seeking advice from those that entice
our fear in which to use
for or against while keeping the stance
there is nothing left to loose

It's been written we see
that one day there will be
an event we dare not be found sleeping
for in that moment with the blink of an eye
that thief in the night will come reeping

Taking those ready that held their faith steady
to their reward for stayng awake
what will be our final saving grace
that all will wear upon their face
the love of GOD bestowed upon those he calls home
into that time of eternity upon which his will be done

One simple thought

perry d sisk--feb025

Well one day with nothing particular to do
I look down and saw I needed to tie my shoe
I set out walking down this dry old dirt and gravel road
Not knowing where it led i've stepped in and out of ruts
where once some water flowed
It must have been a mile or so
I thought to stop and rest
I sat down in some weeds
That Were two feet high at best
I closed my eyes to take it all in
what sounds of the stillness allowed for and then
Something said get on my feet
And start walking more again
so as I stepped back on this road
I see as being less traveled
The dirt on which I walked I saw
was becoming far less graveled

I began to feel a sense of peace
I knew so long ago
As if I'd stepped far back in time
To a point that only the older would know
There were no noises of planes in the air
Or any cars with engines racing
Only the thoughts of that more gentle time
What my mind said I was facing
There is no mystery to what I've been allowed to see
All the reminders of A simpler time
So longed for no longer to be
Being at a loss to ever understand the reasons for it all
Far easier to say We had to have heard the call
That call to realize We have all held a purpose
Some early on and some of late
Blown away are the memories we hold
Given to upend our fate...............

One true faith

perry d sisk--feb025

Is it odd how we see time and time again how the young

Wish to be older not yet knowing what has been

and then as the coin is turned the older wish that they were young

And giving up those things they learned

So then too What falls too late

Open our minds determine fate

What goals set forth to achieve or debate

Yet in some ways set an empty plate

One old way of saying there's too much going on

you got too many irons in the fire

Is this what keeps you strong

I was also tall not to Buffalo my way into thinking

Of course this way of talking now

these others eyes a blinking

though still the essence of these generations past are really not too distant

To get to where we're headed all too quick and fast

so in these thoughts I've written down

I hope we'll shed some light

On wisdom found from those that walked on older ground

endured one longer fight

Always on the edge of just learning something new

this applies to all still living those young or old or who

just who is always giving

In faith our faith is true.....

One truth never lost

perry d sisk --jan025

Always within the writing of a novel
or merely a book of poem
And as with all that is sought for be it insight
Up or one glimmer of wisdom
That brings us back home
Some ever realize or ever come to know
Why just how or even when
They may cast their Inner Glow
As the sapling of a tree we see
Was yielded from one single fruit
Of which belonged to one more older
As Sands beneath our feet astute
Of all the Deeds that carry over
To be deemed as lessons for others
Reflected upon though so often passed on
To our fathers and our mothers
For anyone and all who is listening here

That know there is more to tell
Why it goes without saying the numbers
That will be praying
When there is no more living water in the well
And too it is said that truth always prevails
Just as a ship on the sea is still
seemingly with no sails
Given these facts like science of today
Was seen as magic of the past
What a future holds or will present
To any should Humanity be allowed to last
Lasting Beyond a foreseen end
Which no man can ever know
Forever declared by one alone
One past, one present,,
One future may show
In knowing what has been
And seeing what is and hoping what may be
From that bush on that mountain that burned
Whereby our Salvation so earned
By faith from you and me.........

Our light to see

by--perry d sisk--October O24

If it is true when we meet our demise
That light of our spirit once seen in our eyes
Where has it gone why was it there
As a tone in a song
That held Joy or despair
It's been said that our eyes
Are the windows to the soul
When that twinkle Fades away
Is when grief and sorrow take hold
These times come about
So many times go without saying
It speaks to always rely on
Well past the time for praying
But what if just once
those eyes with light returned
Could we say there was Providence
We wish before we had learned

No one can say or ever foretell
Just when our jobs are through
This time on Earth a teaching ground
For when we're called home and too
This light in our eyes not solely meant
If not for Just To See by or through

Question for a poet

perry d sisk

How often do we find
Ourselves wishing we'd done it better
No particular one thing
Or even words we use in a letter
Many times throughout our lives
And in so doing for fortune sake
We let go of those hearts we mend
No one can ever say
They were never guilty of the same
For in repeated efforts
On who we cast the blame
I too confesse with some degree
Of duress to fall into this group
Regardless what tore this fabric I wore
That show how low some will stoop
All for the sake of holding what is fake
And kept from others' view

Are there more that will claim
They have failed in doing the same
We'll hold fast to all that is true
Is it now time to quit
there are my pen and paper will set
To collect the dust of time
No longer an interest
It has all been done in jest
Two put thoughts out that do rhyme..........

Reason for why

If folks could entertain the thought that our lives we have lived were just for naught

Then would we have to ask for what purpose has it been just one more instance by chance we got?

If the living holds no purpose why is life givin then

If just to see and be observed by the spirit of we never see but counts those ways we sin?

It's been said before and will be spoken of again

The whys and what fors we hold within

Being tested throughout what we endure

Who outlives who defeats the Allure

Of having life and in and of itself was never our choice to make

So indeed something or someone else

Holds that power to give and take

For myself I come to conclude this life this world is preparation

For what does lie ahead

There will be no comparison to all we know

Now and can't conceive of as we part our mortal self it is said.......

The Rarity of all

Perry d sisk --- October 024

Where do words of wisdom come from
Are they far away as the sun
Would could I do it all again much in
the same as some would I ask
Some will say there's not enough time in a
day to accomplish all we are tasked
Too As I have known the many times I hear it said
Let's don't and say we did
Get it passed move on instead
Can't lay claim on knowing very much
In ways that some would aspire
To always keep in touch
It is no secret we have all used poor judgment in our lives
So this Testament is true why some
women leave their husbands
And some husbands leave their wives
What has always been known though rarely shown

We're given to Mortal Frailty
One thought in conclusion
Apart from illusion
Does speak of itself and our Rarity

The will to tell

perry d sisk -- October 024

Think for a moment
Going back to Creation
The reason for free will
And why we are prone to hesitation
Suppose that our father himself
Took all his time to reason
He weighed the pro's and disparagement of
A world that held no season
For those that deflect their eyes
From the beauty that was placed in what lies
Be to extend between all we see as was his plan
If not by Design Pick A Part if we can
These mistakes that we make some atoned for and shared
Leaves so little to repeat that very reason that we cared
This Free Will we've been given
Will go one of two ways

Want to admonish and one it so sways
One Direction we take that can lead to his glory
Those ends and outs of Our Lives
That reveal our true story......

This kinship to others

perry d sisk----oct 024

Of things I see of this world today

Often make me turn my eyes away

How many times can I say this I find

Some seem to be soulless and all too often blind

There are things we think of

That alter our Direction

To only find a means to an end

That cannot Escape one closer inspection

To travel through life in a world some call illusion

Dare we to ask what is best kept in seclusion

For those that aspire to be who they are not

Lends others to ask for what purpose they fought

Each and every day we arise and take heed

For the wisdom we gain yet see others in need

Some that hold a sharper Whit

Have clever metaphor to pick and choose

Such as that dog won't hunt or there is little to gain

Or so much more to loose

We all I guess do think of words to pass along to others

Or more to say we all have our druthers

Relative or not we should love all our brothers......

This time we miss

Perry d sisk -- October 024

Things that I see that time sweeps away like hair growing thin
and what remains turning gray

Just as the sun will set upon the ending light of day as a
conversation ends for lack of more to say

Time will still move on regardless of event

 though still we all account for things our time was spent

With adversity and achievement running always at odds

there will be that point in time itself

That separate Greeks from gods

What is seen as the master of Our Fate and of our dreams

Also known as Relentless with no constraint it seems

If learning from our past can be viewed as wisdom gained

So then too a desert sand does dismiss the clouds that rained

So in an end this time we spend no words will ever offend

So invision this for who we miss captured up with time again.......

This we share

perry d sisk--October 024

As days go by that I watch as they fold upon each other
I see the sunrise and I watch it set
The light of day to smother
Given this to be a constant there is no argument for
So and too a knock we hear
We fear who is at our door
Sitting alone amidst the silence
With no one to share a view
I see as chance to make use of the space
To gather thoughts anew
You know the beauty of an entire day
It can be seen in what folks can simply say
One simple I miss you or I wish you were here
And I wish that you could stay
So simple yet deeply felt our thoughts when left alone
They take us down and lift us up and still we cast a stone
Into a pond or down a well and make a wish for more

More of the same we bare resistance for
what makes us walk the floor
And this I find as others will some soothing balm to heal
Those wounds we've carried throughout our lives
And those we feel so real.............

What was and then

perry d sisk--October 024

There are times we have to ask just when did it all change
Those teams of stallions Mustangs and bison
Upon an open range
Folks never gave a second thought to
open doors for one another
As an old mother hen protects her chicks
The same regard for the other
A school week would end with a couple days to spend
And rest for that Monday ahead
And the blink of an eye that time would go by
To do it all again instead
People would meet on this traveled Street
and smile and Shake Your Hand
This too has changed it's all rearranged
With no one knowing just where to stand
Things you used to be so simple to see
As the blue on a cloudless day

Now as it rains we wonder what stains
we will find along our way
I hear people say There's No Going Back
And to change we'll be better for it
But in my own Mind's Eye there is more to lack
Like a puzzle with pieces that just don't fit
So this picture I'm seeing nowadays finds me wishing
For what has been
Those days we took things all in stride
We hope will return again.and then..........

what was may be again

perry d sisk -- October 024

there are things that we see there are no words to Define
like birds and foul that migrate south
know how to keep in line
When We Were Young didn't Folks ask
what our goal in life would be
then of course while so much to wonder
just how much would there be to see
we learn early on as we all recall and know
that a friend in need can become a friend indeed did show
old school days along with old school ways
taught us that a Garden of Good and better things
does come about with just one seed so planted it stays
with reflection to our past did we hope that hope would last
for in this we find that cause to move on
keeping faith and staying strong
as walking through a pasture beyond the crest of a hill
that pond I had fished from I recall so clear and always still

I would wish to return to that time again
that touch of serenity
perhaps the other side will hold
what was for all eternity......

Words in one book

Perry d sisk -- Dec 024

For all who wander or question

For what their purpose has been given

Could it be as simple to see

What impression we have on others still livin

Reach back on our past to recall a light we did cast

On which we chance to change

Our Visions were blurred by those songs that we heard

The pitch of which was strange

Why was it said that music can charm a Savage Beast

Knowing full well we can't simply tell

The bread to rise with no yeast

So just think for a moment how easy it has been and I don't know where this comes from

And I cannot say to whom I would lend

All of our trains of thought seemed to switch their track

Just when we find an answer sought for

We then will throw it back

Are now look at things that could have been

And see all things done wrong

I see you in dreams what should be now

Yet find no lyrics to this song

A song Once sang among those once I knew

That take my thoughts back where memories were few

To a time and a day where peace seems so apparent

With a closed line in our yard a breeze through some roses yielding their scent

These many years I have lived giving things to contend with

As on an ocean of Dreams alone and so adrift

I often wonder are there any more chapters left in this book

Adjacent to his word laid out

For all to take one look